Thoughts Ensconced

A Book of Poetry

Inna Couri

BookLeaf Publishing

India | USA | UK

Dedication

for the voice in my head
the people who inspired dread
and a very dear friend

Preface

these are some poems
that i had written down in my notes

a friend of mine challenged me
and so now i share them for all to see

twenty-one was all that i could include
so i simply picked my favorites for this debut

there is no specific order for this jotted poetry
a random assortment like how these thoughts come to
me

speaking my mind is not always what i want
so written down here are my thoughts ensconced

Acknowledgements

I want to acknowledge my dearest Nightengale, without whom this book would not exist. Thank you for always letting me share my thoughts with you and for encouraging me to share with others too. Thank you for helping me create this book and for being my sounding board in all things. Most of all, thank you for being a great friend.

myself the most

i think i like myself the most
when i sit down and turn my thoughts into poems
put things down in my notes
and become someone you and i
might not know
an artist
a dreamer
a soul who's been beaten down and damaged
someone who has endured
more than what has actually happened

don't you know the fun
of becoming someone
who's head is in the clouds
without a foot on the ground?
the ideas in my head
are more beautiful somehow
when it's love and war
and profound sadness and lore
turning an emotion
into more
than just that
into a story
something that's about me

but also maybe not really

can't you agree
that there's something so unique
about us all
when we let our minds run free
and not have to think sensibly
about all of life's woes
all those things that get in the way of creativity

it kind of feels like nobody
these days
really escapes reality
and just exists in poetry
which is sad to me
because this is where
i like myself myself the most
when i sit down and turn my thoughts into poems

daydreaming

i don't know how or why
but you have been occupying my mind
all day and all night
ever since we said goodbye

and i don't even want to try
to stop imagining you are mine
because you are like the moon
lighting up my dark sky

like a light

i'm like a light
that's running out of life
i feel dim
like there's nothing within
me that wants to grin
i can't swim
i'm drowning
i can't keep my head up
i can't win

but
i know i'll be all right
because
like a light
i can be turned back on
brought back to life
there are times when it's dark
and then later i'll be bright
sometimes i'm warm
with orangey hues
and sometimes i'm cool or blue
sometimes i'm harsh
like a fluorescent
and sometimes i'm just beautiful

radiant, incandescent

there are so many ways
you can see me
so many ways i can be
and that's part of the beauty
i can change
i'm not always the same
i'm like a light
i feel dim
but i'm going to be all right

limerence

limerence
a word
i hadn't heard
until now
but a state
i've been in somehow

it describes
the uncertainty
i have in me about you
the knot
my stomach turns into

it is my obsession
i never volunteered
how my mind
cannot be cleared

it is the way
i can't see anything
without also seeing you
and the way i'm blue
because you don't see me
you just see right through

growing

this is the season where i plant my seeds
no one knows yet who i'm going to be
i'm growing in the dark, focusing on me
it takes time to bloom and no one sees
what goes on in between

but that's actually where you'll grow the most
and your efforts soon will be noticed
and by the time you are a beautiful flower
you will realize that all your power

actually came from the mountain
that you had climbed
not the beauty that's on the outside
but who and what you found within
when you were growing in the dark
that was the real win

cold

each day and each night
i am greeted by

a wicked, frigid envelope
that chills straight to the bone
slithering around me
hunting for the warmth down to my soul

the air cackling, howling
the sound ever taunting
like a witch brewing a potion
planning her reviling

seeking to steal
a thief in the night
i shiver, defenseless
like a sleeping child

i succumb to the power
my body cowers
only panic and despair left
losing willpower

no sign of hope

no fire to stoke
will i ever be able
to escape the cold?

thinking about you

i try to imagine you sometimes

where you are
what you're like
are you all alone
or is there someone by your side?

are you shadows and darkness
or shining bright?
are you far away
or close by?

are you sleeping well
or tossing and turning at night?
are you thinking of me too
what's on your mind?

and how will we meet
when will you be mine?

the girl in the picture

as i look at two images of me
one from four years ago
and the reflection i see

i can see the exuberance and zest for life
has ever so left her eyes

time has done a number on her
she has less of herself left to share
somehow impaired, pitiable when you compare

the world was her oyster
and now she is just a shell
once bright-eyed and bushy-tailed
but now where is her will

like a glass that has been spilled
there isn't even half of it to fill
from one hundred to nil
a slope only going downhill

her face is more gray
once bright like the whole sun
and now hardly a ray

she used to flourish
but now is decaying

something has jaded her spirit
can't you see it?
she used to be whole
and now there's a pit
passionate and persevering
but now where is her grit?

a vibrant light
that has faded
a fire in her eyes
that has been taken

how many ways can i admit?
that i'm not the same
i'm different

still dying to be, trying to appease
but i'm just a bad parody

i wonder if there's anything left
any similarities
between the girl in the picture
and the one looking back at me

just someone

i long for just someone
anyone
tonight
because i am alone
but I know in the long run
i'd rather wait
than waste time
with the wrong one
with someone who doesn't belong
if they're not meant to be here
don't string them along
just to say
you have someone
you can wait
until it's great
don't make the mistake
of thinking
you won't be okay
you will
even if it's hard
this is just part
of the journey
you can't hurry
something like this

don't be foolish
don't waste
your love
because
don't you know
it will end in heartbreak
don't you want to save
more hearts
from not being whole?
you know
how it feels to be
in that hole
but then then again
i'm already in a hole
so maybe
i can go
with just someone
anyone
because i am alone

you called me

you called me that night
begging on your knees
come get me, please
you said
i can't take this anymore
i need you to set me free

it was at this time
all the emotions i tried to freeze
came rushing back to me
and ever since that night
i have not been all right
i couldn't give you what you plead
and it broke me

back to you

looking at the color blue
isn't just sad or melancholic
it's torture
because all i can see are your eyes
all i can think about is you

and hearing someone say your name
doesn't just leave my mind a mess
it's like someone is grabbing hold of my heart
and ripping it out of my chest

the eye of the beholder

when you see it the way i do
it looks rather beautiful

but you might not think so
and ultimately i know

beauty is in the eye of the beholder

and that's all right
there's no need to cry

if you worry about the beholders
who don't see it the way you do
it will just drain you
and it won't change their point of view
or make it more beautiful

so i don't worry about anyone beholding
the things i see
i just appreciate
what's beautiful to me

haunted

i look at the clouds over the moon
haunting
like every time i think of you

that's where my mind goes
it's all i'll ever do

it's all i've ever done
because you were the one
you were my sun
how could another
ever give me as much?

do you know how i loved you?
do you know what you've done?

you've taken everything from me
i can't sit or think or hardly breathe
all i can do for the rest of time is weep
i'm just a sliver of who i used to be

i don't look like me
i'm haunted
you're haunting me

it was God

it wasn't him rejecting me
it was God saying he wasn't worthy

and it wasn't me not being enough
it was God steering me from the wrong one

it wasn't me not catching his eye
it was God knowing where i shouldn't lie

and it wasn't him not knowing what he had
it was God guiding me with his own hand

it wasn't him making me feel low
it was God telling me where i shouldn't go

and it wasn't me making myself sad, dwelling on the
past
it was God reminding me of what i had learned, to not
go back

it wasn't me knowing who was right or wrong
it was just God all along

like a sunset

i was once a ray of sunshine
radiant and bright
but then i allowed you to see me
like a crystal ball, beautiful and whole and vulnerable
but while I allowed you to see me, you weren't really
looking
you carelessly mishandled me
i was dropped onto a cold, hard concrete floor
shattered into a million little pieces
but what's more, is that people still think i am the ray of
sunshine
expecting me to shine bright for them
so i am shining on with what's left of the scattered
pieces
instead of getting put back together
and hoping they don't notice that i am actually more like
a sunset
fading more with each moment
and even though there is beauty in a sunset
all it really leads to is darkness

the slowest burn

maybe it's the slowest burn to ever exist
or maybe it's limerence
maybe you think about me sometimes too
or maybe i'm just making it up in my head about you
because i want it to be true

how will i ever know?
how could i ever not wonder?
about what i was to you
and if you ever felt that spark too

i'll hold on for the rest of time
wondering if you could be mine
until you admit
that it wasn't limerence
you just didn't know how to say it
you were scared
and that it was
the slowest burn to ever exist

cloudy night

dark clouds race
like horses out of a gate
wordlessly conveying
gloom and doom you might say

through the sky ripping
but an optical illusion
or is it the stars moving
could maybe i be tripping?

a picturesque projection of a midnight sky
an eerie motion picture
my eyes are telling lies
'cause i could swear to you
all the stars flying

moving through the clouds shining
a million shooting stars
like fireworks on the Fourth of July
you can't help but stop and stare

the sky is such a wondrous sight
even on a cloudy night

the space between us

when the space between us shrinks
i can't help but think
about what ifs
and maybe so's

when i'm close enough to you
that i smell your perfume
my mind is anew
with thoughts of me and you

can i say
there are a million different ways
i've pictured you and me...
what if that's our destiny?

if it's not
then why is that all i can think?
i'm losing my sanity
why don't you ever say anything?

have you ever had a thought like that?
have you ever just stopped to think
even for a second
when the space between us shrinks?

wish you were mine

every night there comes this time
when i want to lay down and cry
because there's nowhere to hide
from this lonely feeling inside

i can't help but feel the bitter cold
of being all alone
and maybe it's the absence of daylight
or the way the stars shine
but somehow all i can do in that moment
is wish that you were mine

self-sabotage

when you are
pitying
yourself
you can
blame
the world
and continue to
wallow
while holding
the gun
instead of
looking at
the one
who is in
the mirror

the end

who's to say the end
will be any different?
i've learned that it's hard
at every stage for different reasons

so we can't dwell
thinking one day
there will be this big change
where everything will be great

because
once you get to that day
there will be other things
in your way
things you didn't even know
could cause you to fray
i assure you
that difficulties are here to stay

haven't you heard the saying?
that life is hard
they didn't mean just one part
the whole thing
will have edges that are sharp

and times that are dark

you just have to learn
to find your own light
make the best of the situation
no matter how hard the bite

there might not ever
be that true end you have in sight
where everything is bright
and that's all right

that's just life
learning how to stay upright
no matter what is thrown at you
now or in the distance
because who's to say
the end will be any different?

www.ingramcontent.com/pod-product-compliance
Lightning Source LLC
Chambersburg PA
CBHW071240140726
47996CB00007B/2693